HIGH-STAKES HEISTS

MUSEUM HEISTS

KENNY ABDO

Fly!
An Imprint of Abdo Zoom
abdobooks.com

abdobooks.com

Published by Abdo Zoom, a division of ABDO, P.O. Box 398166, Minneapolis, Minnesota 55439.

Printed in the United States of America, North Mankato, Minnesota.
052024
092024

THIS BOOK CONTAINS RECYCLED MATERIALS

Photo Credits: Alamy, AP Images, Getty Images, Shutterstock, ©ArildV p16 / CC BY-SA 3.0
Production Contributors: Kenny Abdo, Jennie Forsberg, Grace Hansen
Design Contributors: Candice Keimig, Neil Klinepier

Library of Congress Control Number: 2023948548

Publisher's Cataloging-in-Publication Data

Names: Abdo, Kenny, author.
Title: Museum heists / by Kenny Abdo
Description: Minneapolis, Minnesota : Abdo Zoom, 2025 | Series: High-stakes heists | Includes online resources and index.
Identifiers: ISBN 9781098285746 (lib. bdg.) | ISBN 9781098286446 (ebook) | ISBN 9781098286798 (Read-to-me eBook)
Subjects: LCSH: Theft--Juvenile literature. | Theft from museums--Juvenile literature. | Art thefts--Juvenile literature. | Stealing--Juvenile literature. | Robbery--Juvenile literature.
Classification: DDC 364.162--dc23

TABLE OF CONTENTS

MUSEUM HEISTS

While history's greatest painters and sculptors have filled museums with their art for years, some crooks have wanted to empty them!

THE PLOTTING

The word "museum" comes from the Ancient Greek word mouseion, which means "seat of the **Muses**." It was used to describe a place where people could sit and **contemplate**.

Museums have popped up around the world throughout the centuries. They became the homes for the works of famous artists like Leonardo da Vinci and Rembrandt.

THE SCORES

Three crooks hid in a closet at the Louvre in Paris, France, in 1911. The next morning, they stole the *Mona Lisa*. The thieves tried to sell the work to an **art dealer** months later. The dealer called the police. Mona Lisa smiled again when the thieves were arrested.

The Montreal Museum of Fine Arts was robbed in 1972. Using a broken skylight, robbers tied up the guards on duty. They took 18 paintings worth $2 million. Only a few pieces have been recovered.

In 1990, the famed Isabella Stewart Gardner Museum in Boston, Massachusetts, was robbed. Two thieves posing as police officers broke into the museum.

They **fled** with 13 works. The crime remains unsolved. The artwork from the heist is believed to be worth more than $500 million.

Two thieves broke into the National Museum in Oslo, Norway, in 1994 on the opening night of the Winter **Olympics**. They stole Edvard Munch's *The Scream*. The crooks left a note thanking the museum for its bad security. The piece was found two years later and the thieves were **apprehended**.

The *Portrait of a Lady* was stolen in 1997. After 22 years, a gardener discovered the missing $66 million painting in a garbage bag behind a wall. The Galleria d'Arte moderna Ricci Oddi had its lady back.

Thieves took $45 million worth of paintings from the Nationalmuseum in Stockholm, Sweden, in 2000. They wanted money for the art. The police later arrested the robbers, but only recovered one of the paintings.

The Whitworth Art Gallery in Manchester, England, was hit in 2003. Three famous paintings by Picasso, van Gogh, and Gauguin were stolen. They were **valued** at $8 million. The art was discovered hidden in a public toilet. No one was caught for the crime.

Bandits stole Henry Moore's two-ton *Reclining Figure* statue in 2005. It was worth $18 million. The police never caught the crooks. They suspect that the piece was melted down for metal.

A COVID-19 lockdown heist in 2020 saw the theft of a $6-million van Gogh painting. The thief broke into the Singer Laren Museum in the Netherlands using a sledgehammer. The artwork was **anonymously** returned in 2023 inside a blue Ikea bag.

THE GETAWAY

Millions of people pass through museums every year. They look to the art in search of beauty, truth, and meaning. But some people only see dollar signs hanging on the walls.

GLOSSARY

anonymous – given, created, or carried out by a person who wishes to be unknown or whose identity can't be discovered.

apprehended – caught and placed under arrest.

art dealer – a person or company that buys and sells works of art.

contemplate – to think about deeply and seriously or look at carefully for a long time.

fled – quickly ran away or escaped.

Muse – any of the nine Greek goddesses of the arts and sciences.

Olympics – the biggest international athletic event held as separate winter and summer competitions every four years in a different city.

value – set or guessed the worth of.

ONLINE RESOURCES

Booklinks
NONFICTION NETWORK
FREE! ONLINE NONFICTION RESOURCES

To learn more about museum heists, please visit **abdobooklinks.com** or scan this QR code. These links are routinely monitored and updated to provide the most current information available.

INDEX